MAGNUS CARTER has an international reputation for media and crisis communications consultancy and training. He began his journalistic career with a news agency based in North East England where he provided stories for most national newspapers, later completing his National Council for the Training of Journalists diploma at the Evening Chronicle and Journal in Newcastle upon Tyne.

His subsequent broadcasting career began with one of the first commercial radio stations, Radio Forth in Edinburgh, followed by the BBC's Radio 4 Today programme. He also worked as Intake Editor for the leading broadcast news agency, Independent Radio News, and later, as Group Head of News with GWR Radio. Thames TV and TV-AM introduced him to Television news broadcasting.

Magnus was a senior lecturer for five years on the University of West of England's postgraduate diploma course in Broadcast Journalism. In 1998, he cofounded Mentor Communications Consultancy in Bristol, advising clients on a range of personal communication skills including Handling the Media.

He is an associate consultant at Bristol Business School, a visiting lecturer at Ashridge Business School and a member, accredited practitioner and approved trainer for the Chartered Institute of Public Relations.

Illustrations by: Carys Tait

Published in paperback 2012
by Mentor Press
part of Mentor Communications Consultancy Ltd.
www.mentorltd.co.uk

ISBN 978-0-9572243-0-8

Set in 11pt Trade Gothic by Mentor Press
Printed and bound in UK by Whitehall Printing

# Handling the Media!

Everything you need to know to handle media interviews successfully and build positive relationships with journalists.

by

Magnus Carter

I would like to dedicate this book to the many thousands of people who have stood in front of my microphone or camera. Every one of them taught me something about the process of engagement between journalist and interviewee, and this book is a distillation of all that learning.

I would also like to thank my wife and business partner, Tina Coulsting Carter, a constant support without whom this book would never have happened.

# Contents

# Foreword

In the mid-1990s, I presented a weekly news review programme on a London radio station. The programme consisted of a series of 'live' interviews, with people involved in the big stories of the week and experts who might comment on them.

Working with scarce resources, many of these interviews were arranged at the last minute, and I quickly discovered a sixth sense about interviewees as they were ushered into my studio. This sixth sense enabled me accurately to place them in one of two categories.

The first, all too common category was characterised by what my mind's eye could see as a heavy, grey cloak that burdened their shoulders. Across the back, in large fluorescent letters, the cloak bore the legend – ' victim.'

You might think that, as a hard-bitten cynical old hack I would welcome this – the control I might take, the fun I might have. Mostly, though, my heart would sink. The problem with 'victims' is that they simply answer every question as asked making it difficult to get them to say anything interesting. I needed to be agile on my feet to discover the right question to unlock their knowledge. It was hard work, and sometimes close to failure.

The other category of interviewee has a light in the eyes and a set of the jaw that says: "I've got something to say, and I'm clear what it is" (though they might also look nervous at the same time). For an interviewer, it's a joy. A few easy-to-formulate questions bring forth good information, an interesting viewpoint or a useful reflection.

The truth is that most journalists most of the time prefer to be faced with the latter type. After all, these interviewees can also usually rise to the challenge of a few tough questions, which help makes the interview more entertaining and accessible – and show off the journalist's skills better too.

This book arises out of my passion to share this truth with those who might find themselves at the sharp end of the journalistic process. There is no need to be a victim – indeed, most of the time journalists would prefer you not to be. We actually prefer it if you have something to say for yourself – and of course it's much better for you and for your audience.

More generally, this guide introduces you to the challenging but rewarding processes of media relations. It is designed to show how you and your organisation can cheaply and effectively use the power of the media to your benefit. It is not a definitive guide to Public Relations, a much broader discipline, though it does offer advice on how to take the first steps towards a PR Strategy, which is the essential underpinning for successful media relations.

If you find yourself having to navigate the muddy waters of

media relations alone, without the support of PR professionals, this guide will help get you to your destination safely. If you do employ professional PR support (and you should certainly consider doing so) it will help you manage that support more effectively.

With or without professional support, there is still an important role for the face-to-face encounter with journalists and broadcasters which we call an 'interview.' There is no substitute for practising this skill in the safe environs of training or coaching, but this book is designed to support that practice and to act as an aide-memoire.

The business of journalism has changed a great deal in the past thirty years, and most especially in the past ten. I touch on some of those changes in this book. Yet the basic principles remain the same, and the rules for successful engagement are much the same now as they were when I first started rattling out stories on a Remington typewriter in the smoke-filled newsrooms of the 1970s.

Magnus Carter,
May 2012

A journalist is not interested in you or your message.

The only thing they are interested in is a good story.

So make sure you give them something that's interesting that they can use!

# Chapter 1

## Know Your 'Enemy'

*"Facing the press is more difficult than bathing a leper."* Mother Teresa

When I ask business and professional people how they regard the media, the answers are not usually complimentary. Here are the ten commonest words and phrases they use to describe journalists – you may find they reflect your own feelings:

Adversarial

Devious

Nosey

Untruthful

Unscrupulous

Have their own agenda

Shifty

Untrustworthy

Manipulative

Intrusive

Because of this, most people when dealing with the media tend to be defensive, negative, suspicious and aggressive.

This Guide is not designed necessarily to change your view of journalists. It is, however, designed to inform your behaviour towards them, to the advantage of your business or your profession – and yourself.

**You are not alone**

If you do share the sort of feelings about journalists and the media suggested above, you are in good company. This is what Prince Charles had to say on the matter (and he was talking to journalists at the time!):

> *"Awkward, cantankerous, cynical, bloody-minded, at times obtrusive, at times inaccurate and at times deeply unfair and harmful to individuals and to institutions."*

All of which is enough to put most people off ever dealing with the media if they can possibly help it. And that's especially true of managers and professionals in smaller organisations which cannot necessarily afford extensive support from Public Relations advisers. Which raises an important question:

**Why bother?**

Well there are some very good reasons. Appearing in the media does some things that no other kind of publicity can do, and it also supports all the other kinds of selling tools you use.

- Because it's FREE publicity. It gives you *presence*.

- Because someone else controls the final message, so it's a third-party endorsement for your organisation. It gives you *credibility*.

- Because 87% of people read a local paper and 84% listen to local radio, so you can get your message across to thousands, maybe millions. It gives you *penetration*.

- Because it can advance your career and your company by giving you exposure as an *expert*.

In short, media relations is a tool that creates the conditions in which you can raise your profile and become more successful.

Sometimes, it can even be directly responsible for enhancing sales. When Virgin Direct (now Virgin Money) was launched, a cost-benefit analysis was done on the marketing spend: it found that, pound for pound, the Public Relations effort brought in thirty times more customers than paid-for advertising.

**Why should I get involved?**

Richard Branson offers an answer to that question.

*"I was happy to do anything to increase Virgin's profile: promotion was one of the keys to our growth. If nobody knew about us, nobody would fly us. And if nobody flew us we would go out of business. So, if dressing up in Biggles goggles and lying in a bubble bath helped the airline, I was happy to do it."*

Which is why Will Whitehorn, Brand Development and Corporate Affairs Director for the Virgin Group, says:

*"We've always put it (PR) in the heart of management decisions because we view it not just as a tool for communicating with the media but as part of how we build and grow the relationship we have with our customers."*

**Why does it go wrong so often?**

Usually because being defensive, negative, suspicious and aggressive does not prevent journalists from getting what *they* want, but almost always prevents *you* from getting what you want.

Your relationship with the journalist is not one of buyer to supplier. The journalist is your customer and your contract with them is a *transaction*. There is something in it for you *only* if there's something in it for them – and you need to understand that what *they* want is different from what *you* want.

**So what do they want?**

The commodity in which journalists trade is *news*, and what journalists want from you is a *good story*. They are not necessarily interested in the *information* you want to get across. For the broadcast journalist, there is an additional element – they also need you to be *interesting* and to *perform* well. They are not necessarily interested in the *message* you want to get across.

**This guide will:**

- Show you how to turn your information into a good story.
- Show you how to turn your messages into an interesting interview.

"Journalists
have the
attention span
of a gold fish
and

the
memory
of an
Elephant!"

# Chapter 2

## What makes News?

*"Asking a proper reporter to define a story is like asking a teenager what lust is."* Andrew Marr, '*My Trade*' 2004

*"The searchlight of media coverage is not the even and regular sweep of a lighthouse. It is patchy, dwelling on some rocks only briefly, on others at length."* Douglas Hurd, MP, 1998

Journalists may not be able to define what they mean by "news" and they will talk of having a "nose for news" or "a well developed news sense." This section attempts nevertheless to show what will get – and keep – their attention.

Remember that journalists are professional listeners – but selective ones. It has been said they have the attention span of a goldfish and the memory of an elephant. When they read your press release, or talk to you, they are searching for certain triggers that make them recognise your information as a story.

Journalists often see themselves as honest seekers after the truth – but the truth must be told in the form of a news story. And that word TRUTH is an acronym that provides a guide to what a journalist recognises as news:

**T**opical

**R**elevant

**U**nusual

**T**rouble

**H**uman

Topical: News must be up-to-date so tell us what's happening now. It's also about topical themes – if you can, latch on to things journalists are already writing about. There are fashions in news, as in everything else. In the 1960s Alsatians were always biting toddlers and making news, in the 1980s it was Rotweillers, in the 1990s, Pit Bull terriers. Presumably, Alsatians haven't stopped biting children.

Relevant: The subject you want to talk about may be the biggest event in your organisation's history but the journalist will want to know how it will affect readers. Why should we care? Why is it significant/interesting? For local media, relevant means local.

Unusual: You will need to persuade the journalist that what you have to tell is out of the ordinary. It's worth spending some time to discover this – it's the journalistic version of the marketer's 'unique selling point.'

Trouble: Yes it's true, journalists do like conflict. Sometimes you can use this to your advantage – someone else is the target. At all times you can limit damage, or even 'spin' things in your favour [see Chapter 12: *Crisis and Media Relations*]. And remember, if you don't co-operate, someone else will and you will have missed an opportunity.

Human: Journalists like stories about people. If you can, put people at the centre of your story. If you can't, then at least put people into your story – how many jobs are involved, for example. Best of all, tell the story of an individual: use a Case Study.

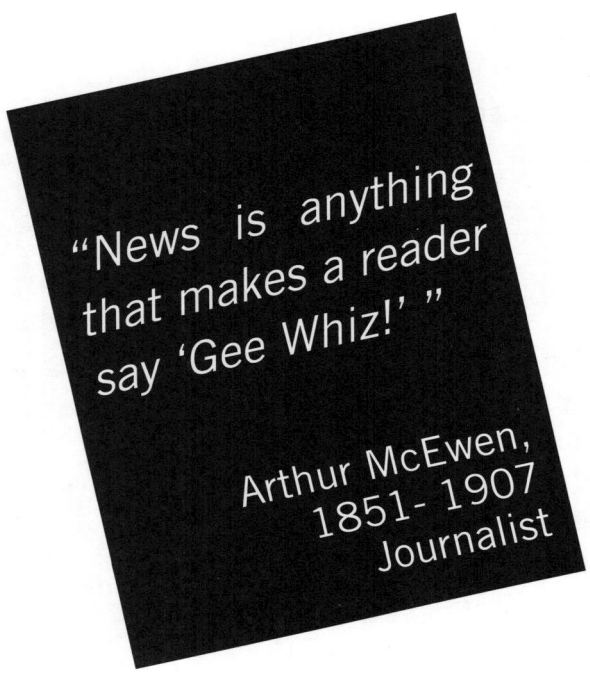

"News is anything that makes a reader say 'Gee Whiz!'"

Arthur McEwen, 1851- 1907 Journalist

**Some say there are only six kinds of news story. Which is yours?**

- Strange but True
- Heroes or Villains (including David and Goliath)
- Tragedy or Triumph
- Row – real, forecast or averted
- Warning
- Hypocrisy exposed

# Alert: Contacts!

Journalists do not have to look very far for a story because they are spoon-fed a lot of material. This means they can be very selective and your story will end up in 'trash' if you don't deliver what they want.  To give yourself an edge, try making personal, ongoing contact with a journalist.

Establish an open communication channel, which will need to work both ways – you need to be ready to give information or help even if it is not necessarily directly to your advantage. You can phone your contact to offer a story or a quote, and get a much better response than you'll get from a formal news releases.

# Alert: Off-the-record!

This doesn't really exist. In some circumstances, you may want to give information without being quoted – this is called 'non-attributable' and is OK provided you get the journalist's clear agreement beforehand. Journalists will protect 'sources'.

Local or trade press journalists, especially, may need to come back to you on a future occasion. Generally, if you build a relationship with them, you can trust them – but always assume that everything you say may be used.

**No such thing!**

# Alert: Complaints!

British broadcasters are required in law to be fair, accurate and balanced. There is no such legal restraint on press journalists. In extreme cases (e.g. Libel) you may have legal redress. There are also the Press Complaints Commission (www.pcc.org.uk) and Ofcom, The Office of Communications (www.ofcom.org.uk). Initially, you can ask the publication for a retraction or correction. However, ask yourself whether any of this hassle is worth it.

You might be better off complaining to the reporter who originally filed the story, and who will probably feel badly about making a mistake – the outcome may well be another story about you (carefully checked this time). Another good option is to write a Letter to the Editor – try not to make it carping or it may not receive the space it warrants.

Corrections are much more easily made, and in a timely way, on websites, and it is always worth quickly pointing out errors made online.

Is it worth it?

# Chapter 3

## Tried and Tested Stories Top Ten Tips.

### Guinness Book of Records

Journalists love superlatives, and it's worth working quite hard to discover them.  The first of anything, but also the longest, highest, shortest (but bear in mind that no story is *unique*).

### Surveys

Whatever your trade or profession, a survey of customer attitudes or lifestyles will always get space, as long as it is unusual or relevant.  Think about all those house price surveys.  Best if you include a quote interpreting the significance of the results (i.e. what does it mean and why should we care?)

### Competitions

These are not so surefire, because they tend to be seen as marketing tools rather than PR opportunities.  But with a little creative thought, they can become news stories too, especially if the prize is unusual in some way.

### Awards

You can invent an award for almost anything.  What about a

'Supplier of the Year'? You will need something physical to hand over (for the photograph). This idea can include giving money or services to charity, but generally that won't be interesting enough in its own right.

### Animals and children
All animals and most children are highly photogenic – and even a toy animal (teddy bear for example) can add picture-appeal to your story.

## New Faces

A good stand by for the business pages of the local press or your professional periodical. Always send a photograph. May get more space if the appointee can be persuaded to say something interesting, or if you can come up with a creative photograph.

## Long Service

The 'gold watch' story can still work, but best if the award itself is a little more unusual, or if the receiver has an interesting story to tell. Reminiscences aren't what they used to be!

## Launch

New services or products can also be interesting – but remember it's usually the people they involve, or how they affect other people that makes them interesting. What does it do for me?

## Anniversaries

A way of achieving sometimes spurious topicality. "It's fifty years to the day since…." Remember that the original event has to be interesting/relevant and you will need to have something new to say or do.

## Personalities

When in doubt, get somebody famous involved in openings and award ceremonies. Be aware that the personality may command more attention than your story. Pity the poor supermarket manager who booked Freddie Starr to cut the ribbon at his new branch on the day *The Sun* ran the headline, *Freddie Starr ate my hamster*: plenty of media turned up, but no-one was interested in the supermarket.

*One of the most famous headlines of all time, 13th March 1986*

# Chapter 4

## Writing a Good News Release

News writing is not like Business Report writing. You need to accept that you are not going to be able to give the whole picture – just the bits that make it a story, plus supporting facts.

You will need to write the story objectively. This means there should be no qualitative adjectives or adverbs. You *can* say something is a *"first"*, but not *"the best."* – and no opinions, unless you are quoting someone.

You will need to write in the third person (even about yourself). This can be quite difficult until you get the hang of it.

**Golden Rules**

- Make sure the headline is short and to the point. Don't waste time being creative or clever – it will be changed anyway [but see *Ensuring your new release stands out* in this Chapter].

- Make sure the first paragraph tells the story and that

the story is one which is attractive to journalists [as noted in Chapter 2: *What Makes News*].

- Use the 'pyramid' style, as shown on the next page. The first paragraph contains the main points of the story – who, what, where, when. Each succeeding paragraph should be of less importance than the one preceding it.

- Use vigorous language. Keep sentences and paragraphs short and simple. One thought per sentence. One sentence (or two) per paragraph. Make every word count.

- Do not use jargon, clichés or abbreviations – though you may use initials, after stating the organisation's name in full. You may need to give a brief popular explanation of some terms.

- When referring to people by name use both forename and surname in the first instance.

- Always try to give at least one useable direct quotation. These should be checked with the person being quoted, and that person should receive a copy of what they have been quoted as saying.

- Keep it brief. 150-250 words is generally enough.

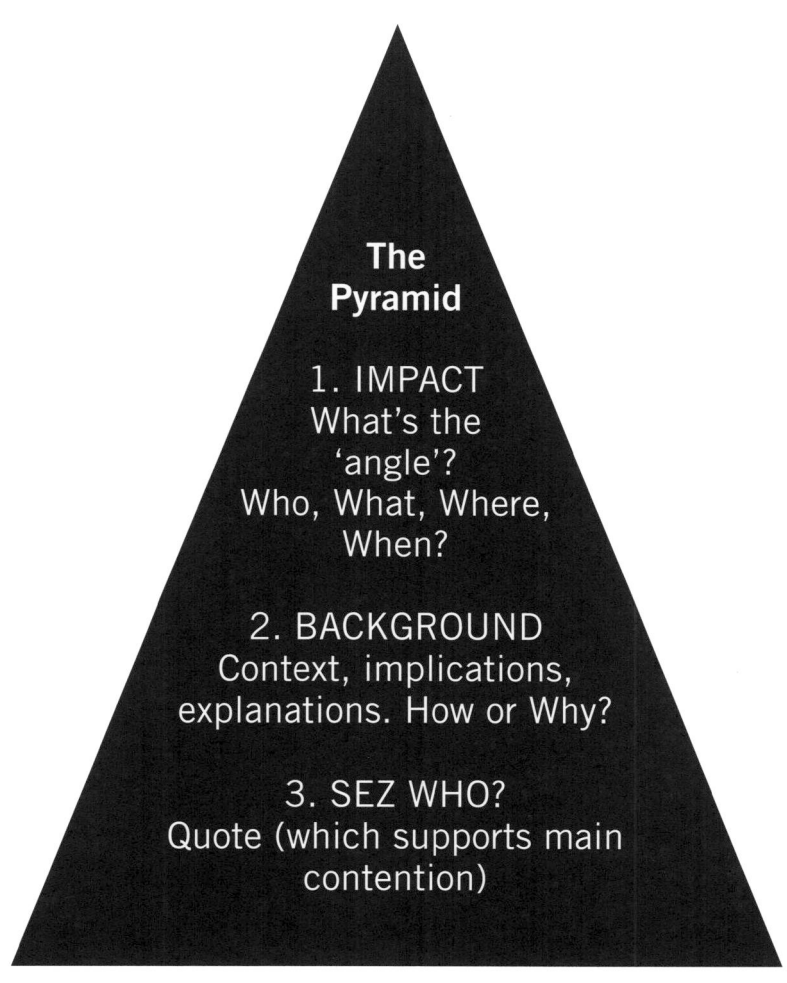

**The Pyramid**

1. IMPACT
What's the 'angle'?
Who, What, Where, When?

2. BACKGROUND
Context, implications, explanations. How or Why?

3. SEZ WHO?
Quote (which supports main contention)

**Presenting your news release**

If the story is a really good one, the News Editor who receives your release may not care how it is presented even if it's scribbled on the back of a napkin. However such stories are few and far between. If you want to get attention for a story which is less than earth-shattering you need to make life easy for the journalist and work within the accepted professional conventions.

All news organisations now expect to receive material via email – the hard-copy press release is pretty much a thing of the past, though it may still have a place in press packs handed out, for instance, at launch events or openings.

**Ensuring your news release stands out**

*At last a decent story!*

- If preparing a hard-copy version, type on one side of the paper only, with large margins.

- If releasing via email, it is generally best to paste the copy into the body of the email. In-boxes get clogged up with attachments, and some systems may reject logos etc. For similar reasons, if you want to send photographs or graphics, check before doing so, send them as separate attachments and send a covering e-mail explaining what you are doing.

- You will be fighting for attention in the journalist's in-box. As often as not, he or she will decide whether to read or delete on the basis of the subject heading of the e-mail, so make it count. Try to capture the excitement of the story in a headline.

- At the end of the release type the word ENDS in capitals after the final line.

- Date the release in full either at the end or at the top.

- The date and time your release can be published should appear at the start of the release:

  If there is no restriction type FOR IMMEDIATE RELEASE. If the release is embargoed, state the date and time of the embargo e.g. EMBARGOED: NOT FOR RELEASE BEFORE 0030 HOURS, FRIDAY 22nd

NOVEMBER, 2013. (Use the 24 hour clock). Do not embargo a release without good reason: these days, embargoes should be used with great caution and will be disregarded by the media unless there is a convincing reason for them.

- If the release relates to a speech or presentation, it may be marked 'CHECK AGAINST DELIVERY', i.e. the deliverer of the speech may make amendments after release. We advise against this usage, unless you are certain the media will actually attend the event.

- Ensure that it is clear who and where the release has come from. Give at least one contact name, with day and evening phone numbers. Make sure the contact will be available when the release reaches the media.

## Photographs

They say a picture is worth a thousand words, and in newspapers and online that can be literally true. A good picture will often occupy more space than a thousand words and be remembered long after the headlines are forgotten. Photographs can add a lot to the impact of your news release. If the picture is strong enough in its own right, you may not need the release at all – just a brief caption.

There are three ways in which newspapers and magazines get their pictures:

- Internal commission of staff photographer or freelance by the News Desk, to illustrate a story.

- Provided 'on spec' by staff or freelance photographers who have an eye for an interesting shot.

- Submitted by external individuals or organisations as a free contribution.

Some local newspapers rely quite heavily on the last category, and most these days will welcome contributions, as will virtually all 'trade' or professional magazines. However, the pictures must generally meet certain criteria:

- Virtually all media outlets will welcome digital pictures submitted by e-mail – but check their technical requirements: if a picture is too big, it may fall foul of email filtering systems which cannot cope with too much data. These days, almost all publications also have websites which need illustration – so even radio stations need pictures.

- If sending prints (never transparencies) they must be good quality – sharp focus and well composed – and large format. Colour is fine as the publication can easily reproduce them in black and white if they wish.

- Pictures should feature people. Sometimes large groups are acceptable, but usually it's best to have no more than five. Products on their own are only interesting to a very limited range of specialist magazines – better if we can see them being used.

- If possible, the people should be doing something. Try to avoid the clichés (like someone presenting someone else with a large, cardboard cheque).

In this digital age, it is easy enough for anyone with an 'eye' for a picture and a decent camera to take an acceptable shot. However, don't cut corners. It's often far better to pay for a professional photographer. Look for someone with newspaper or magazine experience. Most localities have a freelance photographer who used to work for the local paper, knows Picture Editors and understands what 'turns them on'.

**TV pictures**

Television news is a slave to pictures. The more visual the story, and the more *dramatic* the pictures, the more prominence they'll be given.

So, when dealing with television crews your job doesn't begin and end with the interview. You will need an interesting (but not distracting) backdrop for the interview. You will also need to provide access to interesting 'moving' pictures to help them put their piece together. And be prepared for it all to take at least *twice* as long as you think it will.

# Chapter 5

## Never let the facts stand in the way

*"It's the way I tell them."* Frank Carson, comedian

In the media context, the truth of a story is in the selection of facts. That is the game the journalist plays and you need to play the game that way too – otherwise you may become a victim of the process.

Of course it is true that this process can be manipulated to tell half-truths and to give misleading impressions. The point is that you need to be in control of this process – the ethics of your intention is a separate matter, and one for you to know.

If you were involved in producing chemicals, you might wish to make a valid point about the differences between public perceptions of the risk levels in your industry and the real scientific evidence about them. You might present the following facts about one particularly widespread chemical:

- The chemical industry regularly uses this chemical in its processes.

- It is used in significant ways and often features in spillages and other leaks, regularly finding its way into rivers and into our food supply.

- It is a major component of acid rain.

- It contributes to erosion.

- In its vapour state it is a major greenhouse gas.

- It can cause excessive sweating and vomiting if ingested, and accidental inhalation can kill you.

- It has been found in the tumours of terminal cancer patients.

From the above facts, you might assume that this chemical should be strictly regulated or even banned, and that you wouldn't want any of it near your home.

The chemical is dihydrogen monoxide, $H_2O$ – WATER to you or me!

**In the media context, the truth of a story is in the selection of facts. That is the game the journalist plays and you need to play the game that way too.**

# Chapter 6

## The Media: Who does What?

*"The only qualities necessary for real success in journalism are rat-like cunning, a plausible manner, and a little literary ability."* Nicholas Tomalin, war correspondent

A news story will usually pass through many hands before it is printed or broadcast. Understanding the process may help your professional relationship with the media, and cut down the number of disappointing experiences you have.

**The Press**

REPORTERS are the people you will usually deal with. They are very often 'generalists' and start with little knowledge of your subject. They may have had little time to brief themselves before they talk to you. They often face tight deadlines, so stories are produced in a hurry. Spelling, punctuation, incorrect names and even factual errors easily creep in.

The reporter will be looking for an 'angle' on the story, a 'peg' to hang the news story on. If you don't produce one which is acceptable to the journalist they will find one which you may not like, or not write the story at all.

You are most likely to speak to them on the phone, so it is hard to build relationships, and it is easy for them to mis-hear or misconstrue what you say. If they do speak to you face-to-face, it is increasingly likely they will also want to record a video interview for website use: this is part of the multi-skilling increasingly expected of reporters.

THE NEWS EDITOR directs reporters, and takes a large share of the responsibility for deciding what news to cover, and how. They may also be involved in the 'copy tasting' process which means deciding how the reporter's story should be treated once it is completed, including how much prominence it gets. The reporter works to please the News Editor (and not necessarily the reader).

THE CHIEF SUB-EDITOR works closely with the News Editor and either holds or shares the responsibility for story selection and treatment. They will plan the pages, deciding what goes where, how long the story will be, and what deadlines are appropriate for what pages – inside pages are usually printed first. Sometimes important stories receive less prominence than more minor issues just because of deadline problems. The 'Chief Sub' often writes headlines and makes decisions on typography.

SUB-EDITORS are responsible to the Chief Sub for the detailed editing of copy. They may rewrite the reporter's story, cut it and write the headline. They will query accuracy, spelling and punctuation. The sub-editor's job is to attract readers to the

The reporter will be looking for an 'angle' on the story, a 'peg' to hang the news story on.

If you don't produce one which is acceptable to the journalist they will find one which you may not like, or not write the story at all.

story. 'Subs' are space conscious and like short words, active verbs and nicknames. They are ultimately responsible for what appears in print and you are unlikely ever to  meet them: everything is edited away from you.

All of the above may also be involved in producing material for the publication's website, but often there may be a less rigorous checking process in place – for example, reporter's may input directly [see Chapter 2: *Alert: Complaints*].

## Broadcasting

Emphasis is placed on the visual impact in TV and the aural impact in radio. Time is also important. Stories are measured very precisely in minutes and seconds.

## Television

TV REPORTERS often have little influence over the stories that are selected. News Editors will decide, usually at a morning meeting, the items of interest and allocate camera crews accordingly – though 'specialist' reporters (e.g. Political Editor, Health Correspondent) will have an important input into this process. News priorities do change, and sometimes interviewees are approached at very short notice. In general though, reporters and crews are committed early in the day for all but big, 'breaking' stories.

The business of bringing together the reporter and the crew in the right place at the right time is a complex one, even in these days of lightweight cameras, smaller crews, satellite communications and computerised editing.

However, VIDEO REPORTERS are increasingly common, and not just with cable channels – they gather pictures and information and occasionally conduct interviews from behind the camera. The BBC has introduced PERSONAL DIGITAL PRODUCTION (PDP) into Regional Newsrooms: reporters with a small digital camera follow you around over a period of time to compile, in effect, a mini 'fly-on-the-wall' documentary. This presents new and different challenges to those who are the subject of such coverage [see Chapter 8: '*Fly on the Wall*'].

Once the video tape is returned to the studios, the reporter will consult the PROGRAMME EDITOR, PRODUCER or NEWS EDITOR on the story treatment. The technical editing process is usually carried out by a VIDEO EDITOR, working with the reporter, though sometimes this work may be carried out on a desktop by the reporter. They may also record and edit into the soundtrack additional reportage or 'voice over'. The script for this will be written by the reporter, who will also provide an introduction, to be read by the PROGRAMME PRESENTER. The item may be subject to further editing by the PROGRAMME EDITOR or PRODUCER, who may decide at the last minute not to use it at all.

## Radio

RADIO is generally a much simpler process than TV. Decisions on what stories to cover will still be taken by the NEWS EDITOR or the DUTY EDITOR deputising for him/her. In local radio, the same NEWS EDITOR or DUTY EDITOR will often be responsible for compiling, and very often reading, the News Bulletins. He or she may direct the REPORTER on treatment of stories and may rewrite cue material handed in by the reporter for the 'intro' to the edited recording.

Otherwise, almost the whole process is in the hands of the REPORTER – who will conduct the interview, usually without technical assistance, and will also edit the recording and write the cue material. In the case of non-interview material, the reporter will write his/her own reports, which will not usually be subject to further editing.

In national radio, processes may be slightly more complex and may include extra technical assistance like a studio technician to handle the technical aspects of editing.

The interviewer
may have
control of the
interview BUT
you have control
of the subject!

# Chapter 7

## Talking to Journalists: The Interview

*"Journalists say a thing they know may not be true, in the hope that if they keep on saying it long enough it will be true"* Arnold Bennett, author, 1867-1931

**Why you should do the interview**

- To make sure your point of view is aired.

- To help the journalist get the story right.

- If you say "no", you are missing a marketing opportunity.

- If you say "no comment" when your organisation is under fire, this will be interpreted by the audience as an admission of guilt.

**Why the journalist is doing the interview**

- To add value to a story they already have, by giving your version/view.

- To test out that version/view by challenging it.

- To provide illustration to a story.

- To seek a story in what you say.

## What is an interview?

*An interview is a controlled professional conversation between a questioner and an expert on an interesting topic for the benefit of a third party.*

The questioner has the right to control the interview but you, the expert, have control of the subject. Make the most of that. Remember, interviewers actually welcome it when you have something to say for yourself.

It is not an opportunity for you to make a speech, a report, or a dissertation. You must work with the medium and not fight against it. Your aim should be to say, clearly and simply, what you want to say about the subject.

It is not an interrogation. You don't need to answer questions that don't suit you, and you don't need to say anything you don't want to say. You just need to be interesting!

## Why it is essential to prepare in advance

During an interview, you will probably find it virtually impossible to think.  The best you can hope for is to *recall*.  If you wish to recall the right things, it is essential to prepare for the interview. It is also essential to make life as easy as possible for your brain during the interview by keeping things as simple as possible beforehand.

Never be tempted to do an interview without preparation, even if you are very confident in the subject [see Chapter 8: *The 'Doorstep'* and *Press interviews*].  However, deciding what to say should not take longer than about 10-15 minutes – if it does, you may be the wrong person for the job, or you are over-complicating things.

That's not to say that your total preparation will only take 15 minutes.  For an important interview (and you might argue that all interviews are important) you may need a lot longer to reflect, to take advice, to rehearse.  But beware over-complicating things: if this happens, you won't be doing yourself any favours, you risk bamboozling the journalist and – more importantly – you'll lose your audience.  As one of those training acronyms we've all heard of goes – KISS – Keep it Simple, Stupid!

**Singing from the same 'hymn sheet'**

Remember that you can – and arguably should – seek advice from colleagues, especially PR professionals, to ensure your messages and content are in line with organisational thinking. However colleagues will not be able to help in the interview itself, so you will need to be sure you 'take ownership' of what you intend to say: if you don't believe it, journalists will soon uncover that.

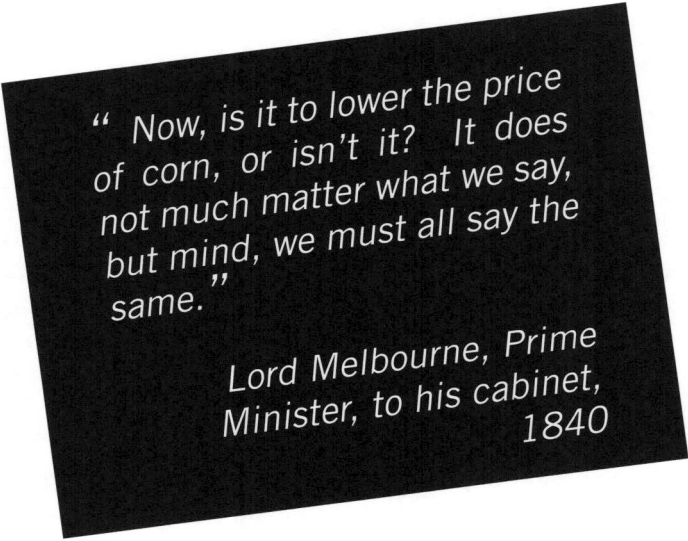

" Now, is it to lower the price of corn, or isn't it? It does not much matter what we say, but mind, we must all say the same."

Lord Melbourne, Prime Minister, to his cabinet, 1840

### Preparation Stage 1: Why me?

As discussed, you will need a very good reason for declining an interview. However, nobody admires a 'rent-a-quote' who is clearly out of his depth. So…

#### Ask the journalist:

- What's the context in which you want to talk to me?
- What is the story as you see it?
- What are you expecting from  me?

**Ask yourself:**

- Why do they want me?
- What's in it for us?
- Am I the right person? (If not, get someone else)

## Preparation Stage 2: How to work out what to say

As in so many things, preparation is the key to media interview success. As the old saying has it, *fail to prepare* and you may as well *prepare to fail.*

In a media context, however, beware the danger of over-preparing. You need to keep your mind clear, to focus on what is really important. We might say AMEN to that! And that's a good way to remember how to approach the task at hand.

### The AMEN approach:

Audience: Start with the audience. There are important differences between listeners to, say, Radio 1 Newsbeat and Radio 4 Today; between a BBC Wales viewer and a BBC World viewer; or between a Business Breakfast viewer and a Watchdog viewer. Issues of age, ethnicity, location, and even education may be important. If you don't know the programme or the station, ask advice about this.

Try to understand as much as you can about your audience's

likely concerns, attitudes, values and needs. Always bear in mind one important common factor: most of your audience, most of the time, will not be paying very close attention – they face too many distractions.

Message/s: You need to have something to say. Once you know your audience, you can start to make some sensible decisions about what you need to tell them – and you are pretty well guaranteed to be interesting, because what you say will be relevant to the audience.

Bear in mind the biggest constraining factor of all in a media context is the limited time/space that's available, so don't have too much to say. How much is too much? Well, anything more than *three key points* will go straight in one ear and out the other (even if it survives the editing process). Ask yourself this question: What are the two or three most important things I must say to this audience about this topic? Apply your expertise to prioritising these points, too – there may not be time to say all you want to say, even now, and you need to ensure the most important message survives: many of the most successful interviews have *one* clear, central message.

Evidence: The trouble with making points or transmitting messages is that – well, you would say that wouldn't you? If you want to be credible – and memorable – you need to *illustrate* your points in some way. This is your evidence, and it may consist of supportive facts or figures: however, it is often more effective if your illustrations have a human dimension –

that's to say case studies, imagined scenarios or anecdotes.

You demonstrate your expertise best by sharing your experience with the audience: after all, that's why they (and the interviewer) wants to hear from you in the first place, and it's why you have much higher status than 'a spokesperson.' So, relevant personal anecdotes are at least as powerful as killer statistics in this context.

Negatives: Up to now, we haven't even begun to think about the *questions* we might be asked. That's because worrying about the questions is not helpful – after all, you can't control that. However long you spend thinking about this, some of them will turn out to be questions you didn't expect, asked in an order you didn't predict, from a perspective that surprises you. However – and this is an important proviso – it may help if you spend time trying to identify the negative 'devil's advocate' questions you may face. Usually, they will be totally predictable (you will know the sort of things opponents of your position tend to say).

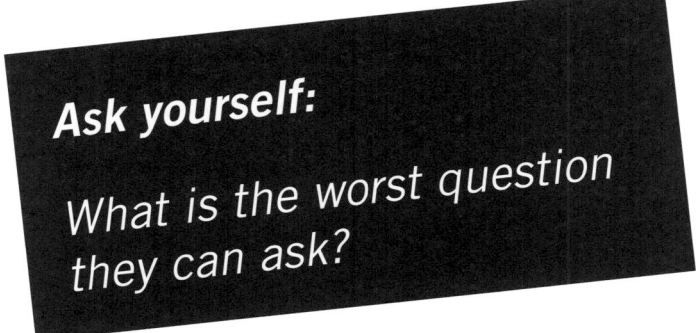

Ask yourself:

What is the worst question they can ask?

**Preparation Stage 3: Rehearsal**

If there is an opportunity to get a colleague or mentor to put you through your paces, take it. If not, do try to practice your soundbites out loud, at least three or four times, so that they are familiar and easily recalled. [see Chapter 9: *Soundbites*]

**In the Interview: What can you say?**

> *"There is no such thing as a wrong question – only a wrong answer."* Ed Murrow, American broadcaster

From a journalist's perspective, you can say whatever you like in an interview, as long as:

- It is interesting.

- It is relevant.

- You accept that the interviewer may challenge what you say.

Always accentuate the positive, and remember:

- You don't have to give a balanced view.

- You don't have to tell the whole truth (though never tell a lie – you may seem to get away with it, but it will come back to haunt you).

**A**udience

**M**essage

**E**vidence

**N**egatives

### How to Take Control: The ABC Rule

During the interview, you need to employ active listening skills. You are listening to the question to see what there is in it that provides a cue or a link to whatever you want to say. The process goes like this:

### Acknowledge

You can say "yes" or "no", you can decline to answer, you can describe the problem, or you can analyse the situation. Often, it will be best to give a direct answer. However, keep this part of your response as brief as possible.

### Bridge

If you can spot a good link, go for it. Select a word or phrase from the question to highlight. Otherwise, use phrases like "That's a real concern, which is why…" or "I understand people may think that, but…" or "What you say is important, but even more important is…" [see this Chapter: *Building Bridges*].

### Content

Use the bridge to reach your own prepared agenda. Say something you planned to say, then shut up. This will give you control of the interview content and should change the direction of the questioning itself (it's the interviewer's job to draw out or to challenge what you say).

# Acknowledge

# Bridge

# Content

## Note

It may sometimes be acceptable to use 'route 1' in responding to a question – i.e. answering a slightly different question from that asked – going straight to your Content. This may be vital where you are asked a 'nutcracker' question which is unanswerable, e.g. "Can you guarantee this will never happen again?" – where your answer means you are damned if you do and damned if you don't.

You may also use 'route 1' when responding to an awkward question that you really did not expect – after all it may be unsafe to make a snap decision on an answer, and the safest thing is to buy time to think, while at the same time saying something you planned.

**In media interviews the rules of normal polite conversation do not apply because only the interviewer gets to ask questions – don't try to turn the tables!**

Generally, do no allow yourself to be interrupted if you are trying to complete an important point – just keep talking, the interviewer will soon shut up.

It is **OK** to repeat yourself – in fact, it's pretty well essential if you want the audience to remember anything.

## Building Bridges

When you can't or won't answer the question use the bridging technique. Here are some classic bridges:

*"Yes, but the important thing to remember is..."*

*"Whatever the rights and wrongs of that, I believe..."*

*"Let's put this in context…"*

*"That's a fair point, but what we also need to consider is…"*

*"That's a very valid question, but the message we need to get across is…"*

*"I understand that many people do believe that, but…"*

*"That's not for me to judge, but what I do know is…."*

*"You might think that, but I believe the most crucial issue we face is…"*

*"That's not the real issue here. This is really about…"*

*"That's true, but more importantly…" (as in: "You're right, this is a great triumph for me, but more importantly, it proves how vital Lottery Funding has been for my sport.")*

*"I can't answer that question (because...), but what I can tell you is..."*

*"I'm not the right person to answer that, but what I do know is this:.."*

*"Before I answer that, let me just say..."*

OR

'Borrow' some of the interviewer's words and re-apply them, as in:

Q: *Can you guarantee this will never happen again?*

A: *What I can guarantee is that we've done everything in our power...etc.*

Q: *Isn't this rather worrying for you?*

A: *What is worrying is that...etc.*

## Anticipating questions

It is a good idea to anticipate questions. But only do this after you have prepared your agenda. It will help you because you can begin working out in advance how to turn the question to your advantage, using the ABC Rule.

Most 'awkward' questions are entirely obvious, if you think about it from an audience point of view (which is what the interviewer will be doing).

## Awkward questions

A useful rule-of-thumb for dealing with awkward questions is:

- Where a *General* question is asked give a *Specific* example in your reply.
- Where a *Specific* question is asked give *General* answer.

Thus…

> *"I can't speak for the industry as a whole, what I can tell you is what my own company does…"*

and…

> *"This is one customer complaint, and we need to remember we deal successfully with many thousands of customers every day."*

## Tell and Show

Illustrations in the form of examples, anecdotes, stories, case studies etc. are important because they:

- Help bring your points alive, make them more

memorable and more acceptable.

- Give you more to talk about without changing the subject.

- Give an impression of a human being rather than a 'spokesperson'.

Bear in mind that illustrations will not come to you 'on the hoof'. They need to be carefully prepared and this may entail some extra time for research but it is worth it. It will save time in the long run if you compile a 'treasure chest' of stories, case studies, or examples on an ongoing basis, you can dip into when an interview opportunity comes up.

**Consider this!**

**Oxford English Dictionary uses 645,000 words**

**Shakespeare uses 25,000 words**

**Commonly understood 20,000 words**

**The Sun Newspaper uses 10,000 words**

**Keep it Simple**

In general, treat your audience as averagely intelligent 15 year olds. Even when talking to your trade press, do not assume they are all experts.

**The rules:**

- Clear points.
- Simple, everyday language.
- Keep facts and figures to a minimum.
- No jargon.

**Clear**

Beware explanations. Tell me what it does, not how it works. Tell me how it affects me, not why you've done it. Tell me only as much as I need to know to understand what it is you are saying. How would you tell your mother?

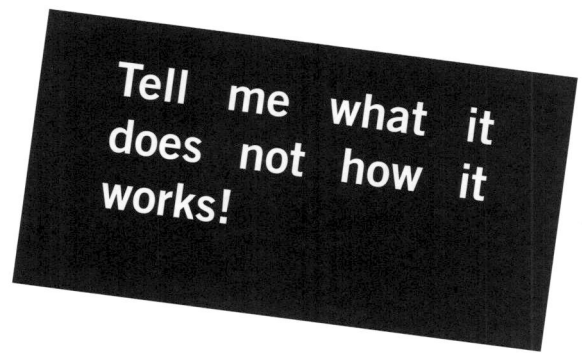

## Simple

Eschew obfuscation!  Use active verbs.  One thought per sentence, with limited use of subordinate clauses or qualifiers.  Use words that people will understand.

## Figures

75% of people don't understand percentages! – So why use them?

What people want to know instead is:  Does it fit in my garage?  How big is it compared to Wembley stadium?  We can visualize "one in five" people, not 20%.

## Jargon

We all know that a Human Resources Development Executive is a Training Manager, don't we?

But would you guess that: *"an accelerated facility restructuring and acquisition integration programme"*, meant 4,000 people were being sacked?

That's a genuine quote from Allen Yurko, Siebe chief executive!

You can have fun making up your own management jargon from the following lists. Choose any combination of words from columns 1, 2 and 3. They will make some kind of sense – but do they actually mean anything?

| | | |
|---|---|---|
| Client-oriented | Input | Evaluation |
| Peripheral | Compatibility | Strategy |
| High-Profile | Awareness | Rationale |
| Multidisciplinary | Viability | Initiative |
| Inter-European | Communications | Function |
| Socioeconomic | Analysis | Package |
| Para-National | Fragmentation | Potential |
| Corporate | Penetration | Spin-off |
| Segmental | Stratification | Criteria |
| Integrated | Database | Infrastructure |
| Demographic | Incentive | Concept |
| Projected | Feedback | Indices |

" Can you guarantee this will never happen again"?

Known as a 'nut cracker' question, how would you answer it?

A good rule of thumb for interviews:

Where a GENERAL question is asked give a SPECIFIC answer.

Where a SPECIFIC question is asked give a GENERAL answer.

# Chapter 8

## Types of Interview

*"Get the game rules sorted out, but remember: the nature of the media is that it's their ball park, it's their ball. It's their game."* John Pike, Shell UK

Media interviews can be broadly classified in two ways (though many will be a combination of bits of both):

**Adversarial:**

- What's gone wrong?
- Who's to blame?
- What happens next?

**Informational:**

- What's happening?
- Why does it matter?
- What happens next?

## Questions you should ask

It is important to know which of the above types of interview you may face, and to find out as much as you can about the interviewer's agenda before you agree to talk at length.

### For all media:

- What's the story as you see it?
- What exactly do you want to know?
- Who else are you talking to?

### If it's a broadcast interview:

- How long will the transmitted interview be?
- Will it be live or recorded?
- Which programme? (Who are the audience?)
- Studio, location, down-the-line or telephone?
- Are others taking part?
- What topics will be covered?
- Can you give me an idea of the first question?

**A good TV interview is 85% dependent on your performance!**

# Broadcasting

*"The medium is the message."* Marshall McLuan, writer

Up to now, we have concentrated on the process of saying the right things. Here comes the disconcerting bit: whether you succeed or fail in getting your message over in a broadcast context is 85% dependent on your performance.

What you say is important. How you say it is vital. If you come across as friendly, authoritative, honest, confident – your message is more likely to be remembered. And, even if the message itself is forgotten, the impression you leave behind will linger.

## First impressions count

In fact first impressions are the only impressions people will receive, unless you are lucky enough to appear on radio and television again and again to the same audience. They will see you and/or hear you for between 10 seconds and five minutes and in that time will form a virtually unchangeable view of you: did you have something to say for yourself, did they trust you? Did they like you?

## Energy and Enthusiasm

These are key to a successful broadcast interview. It is almost impossible to ignore an enthusiastic person. We may not share the enthusiasm, but we can't help but take an interest in it. Think of the media success of Patrick Moore or Andrew Marr.

## Honesty and openness

The bridging techniques discussed earlier need to be used carefully. Politicians use them to avoid having to answer questions which – in the audience's view – should be answered.

Ask yourself: *"Is there any good reason why I shouldn't say this?"*

Unless there is a very good reason, allow yourself to say it. If there is a very good reason – reveal the reason if you can. For example: *"It's a question of customer confidentiality…"* This will engender trust, and make your audience more receptive to your agenda (which of course, you will get to after you have answered the question and built your bridge).

## Anger

You can allow yourself some genuine anger about the subject matter – but beware getting cross with the interviewer. They are there to represent the listener or viewer, and are often regarded as their personal friends.

This is not to say that you need allow yourself to be brow-beaten. Just calmly give your point of view, or if strictly necessary – ask the interviewer openly to allow you to put your point.

# Radio interviews

*"The most important person on any radio station is THE LISTENER."* Michael Bukht, former Programme Controller, Capital Radio and Classic FM.

That's rule number one – know your listner. To understand who the listener is, and how to reach him or her, we need to ask two questions:

### How do people listen?

- People listen alone - not socially.
- People listen while doing something else.

### Why do people listen?

- To be entertained.
- To be informed.
- For companionship.

### So, when you are being interviewed

- Keep it friendly.
- Keep it simple.
- Talk to one person.

**Keep it friendly. Imagine you are talking to one person.**

The process is akin to talking to your neighbour over the garden fence. Use lots of stories – and remember, you need to grab their interest first.

## Be Yourself

Discover and use your own personality. Never imitate others. But be yourself at your best and most interesting.

## Understand your audience

The precise nature and needs of the audience will vary from channel to channel, and even from programme to programme. You need to find out what you can about them. Don't take too much for granted.

For instance, you might assume that a BBC local radio audience is more receptive to your ideas because the station has a high speech content and is therefore 'intelligent.' You might equally assume that a commercial radio audience will not be interested because they only want 'mindless pop'. In fact, in many areas, the commercial station will offer you not only a younger audience but also a more 'up-market' socio-economic mix.

If you can, listen to the programme before your appearance – get a feel for the pace, the approach, the style of the interviewer. You are going to have to fit in with these.

# Television interviews

*" They say 80 per cent of people make up their minds about somebody on TV within 30 seconds. I'd say 90 per cent and 10 seconds!"* Diana Mather, media consultant.

Research shows that viewers retain very little detail of a television appearance and 80 per cent of what they do retain is nonverbal communication – meaning the way you look and sound and how you put your message across.

### Body Language and Nonverbal Communication

Note: The following rules also apply to video interviews for websites or corporate videos.

### Eye contact

This is the single most important aspect of body language. Establish it with the interviewer and maintain it throughout the interview. The camera picks up darting eyes. Viewers will find this off-putting and will not concentrate on what you're saying or may decide to mistrust you. Ignore everything going on around you. And don't whatever you do stare into the camera lens.

Look at the interviewer not the camera!

Eye line may be important too – you don't want to be seen to be looking up (or indeed looking down) at your interviewer. Ask the interviewer or producer to help reduce any disparity in size between you – perhaps by doing the interview seated.

Having said "don't look into the lens", reverse that for 'down the line' interviews. The interviewer will be in a different location, and you need to look directly into the camera lens, which, from the viewer's perspective, becomes the interviewer's eyes.

**Posture**

Make sure you are comfortable before you start. If seated, lean forward, away from the back of the chair, keep hands loose – and use them, if that's natural to you (but keep them away from your face). Otherwise, stay still, do not rock or sway or swivel. If standing, plant feet firmly and comfortably in line with the shoulders.

BBC! Bottom on the Back of the Chair.

**Animation**

Your face (and possibly your hands) can be as animated as you like. Try to look enthusiastic. Practice your open "pleased to be here" smile.

**Appearance**

*General*:
- Wear clothes you feel comfortable in but portray an appropriate image.
- Avoid bold checks or stripes which produce 'strobing'.
- Avoid glasses which hide your eyes, especially light-sensitive lenses.

*Men*:
- Shave before doing an interview.
- Make sure tie knot is neat and jacket lapels straight (and, almost always, wear a jacket).
- Comb hair properly, check for dandruff.

*Women*:
- Normal makeup, no need for more.
- If windy, tie hair up, or wear in short style.
- Avoid flashy jewellery, especially swinging earrings.

To sum up:  Don't be a distraction, and don't be distracted!

**Live or Recorded?**

You will not usually be given a choice.  If you are, it is probably better to take the 'live' option, as it will give you more control.

> **TIP: Stand up for phone interviews – it will remind you that you are 'performing'.**

## Recorded interviews

You have no control over the editing process, so you need to 'score your points'.  Make sure the interviewer can't ignore what you see as the most important issue.  If you can come up with a 'quotable quote' – something pithy or forceful – this will attract the interviewer's attention [see Chapter 9: *Soundbites*].

Don't be afraid to repeat yourself, and keep focused on your key points. If you lose your way or stumble, or find yourself talking your way into trouble, stop and restart the answer.  Better still, ask for the question to be repeated – you can rest assured the hiatus will be edited out.

## 'Live' interviews

Everything you say is broadcast so you don't get a second chance. Adrenalin can help your performance – but you still need to be focused and perform well in order to get the attention of the listener or viewer.  With a little practice, you will learn to recognise when an interview is coming to an end: take the opportunity to make sure you leave the listener/viewer with the point you planned to make.  Be aware that the interview may also be recorded – for further use later in the schedule (e.g. in a news bulletin): in a 24-hour news world, this is increasingly likely to happen.

Recorded or live, it's also important to know the setting for your broadcast interview:

## Studio interviews

The studio environment offers fewer external distractions, and you may find it easier to concentrate the mind. On the other hand, it is an alien environment to you, dominated by technology (but of course 'everyday' to the interviewer). Radio studios tend to be dimly lit, TV studios extremely bright. Don't be intimidated.

## Location interviews

You are on 'home ground' or at worst, neutral territory and therefore may feel more relaxed and empowered. You may also be able to draw on your surroundings, e.g. *"...as you can see behind us, our team are working hard to find the fault..."*

Try to reduce distractions. Take the phone off the hook, turn off your mobile etc.

## Phone interviews

Rare in TV, except for late-breaking news. Very common in radio, especially with commercial stations. If you are used to dealing with people by phone, you may cope comfortably with this one. It will certainly take up less of your time, and inconvenience you very little. However, remember it is still an interview. Prepare properly and follow the rules.

### 'Remote' or 'down-the-line' interviews

This is where the interviewer is in one location, and you are in another – usually unstaffed studios or occasionally outside broadcast facilities. You will be given instructions about what to do, which may even include obtaining a key to get in! You will wear headphones (radio) or an 'ear piece' (TV) and will be alone with the equipment.

This may be daunting if you haven't done it before. TV 'remotes' offer a particular challenge: where to look? The answer is that you need to maintain the illusion of eye contact, from the viewers' perspective. This means you need to gaze into the camera lens, so that your picture on the studio monitor is 'looking at' the presenter.

**Tip:** To avoid giving the impression of roaming eyes fix on a point immediately above the lens (e.g. the red light there).

### ISDN link

Increasingly common, as many organisations have installed inexpensive units designed to link with radio stations anywhere in the world, connecting via ISDN telephone lines. You will wear headphones and speak into a microphone, but will be sitting in an office or bureau rather than a studio. The advantage for the radio station is that they get near-studio quality sound without the inconvenience of booking a 'remote' studio. For you, there is less travel and probably a more familiar environment.

# Variants on the Broadcast Interview

Don't assume that your contribution will necessarily be one-to-one with an interviewer. The following exceptions require special attention to preparation.

### The 'Doorstep'

This usually only happens when the metaphorical wheel has fallen off. If reporters and TV crews are lurking outside your home or place of work, something is wrong and they may try to interview anything that moves.

*Buy time to prepare or risk becoming the 'rabbit in the headlights'*

Remember, you need preparation time. Tell them politely: *"I need to check a few things before I can speak to you"* or *"I'm not the right person to speak to, but I'll try and find someone for you."* Don't say anything you might regret. Turn and walk away: don't run. [see also Chapter 12: *Crisis and Media Relations*].

## 'Fly on the Wall'

Before agreeing to any documentary appearance, you should always seek professional Public Relations advice and make sure all key protagonists have received media interview skills coaching. This is especially the case with the 'fly-on-the-wall' style, in which your everyday activities are revealed.

However, with the advent of Personal Digital Production even daily news coverage can now adopt the 'fly-on-the-wall' approach. This means that anything you or colleagues say or do within range of the camera (which is small and easily forgotten) may be recorded and used.

There are obvious dangers in this. Your preparation needs to include a briefing for all colleagues who might find themselves within camera range. And you still need to prepare your key messages and ensure these come across, even if there is no formal interview session.

## Discussion programme

Most interviews will be one-to-one (called a 'two-way' in the business).  Discussion programmes vary from a three-way (you, the interviewer and another protagonist) to TV's Question Time, with several guests and a live audience.  Make sure you know as much as possible about the others taking part, and their point of view. If it's TV, bear in mind you may be on camera at any time – don't pick your nose!

## Phone-in

Almost exclusively a radio phenomenon.  Phone-ins with guests in the studio will usually be introduced by an interview, carried out by the Presenter.  Sometimes, they may be introduced by a recorded report.  This introductory session may be very brief or quite extended, and it may be carried on at intervals throughout the programme.  The bulk of the programme will be taken up by talking to callers with the Presenter acting as intermediary.  The phone-in is a distinctly different type of experience from any other, and it is worth looking in detail at some of the rules.

### Some special tips for phone-ins:

- The discussion may well be wider-ranging than a straight interview – but you still have an opportunity to make your points.  Go in with an agenda.

- Write down the caller's name and use it.  Talk directly to them.

- Note down the points they raise so you can make sure

you deal with them all and perhaps refer back to them later.

- Be prepared to follow up calls later. If you don't know the answer, promise to get back to them (the radio station will have the number).

- Make something positive out of each call. For example, if a caller has a complaint, point out that such complaints are very rare.

- Be prepared. Check with colleagues beforehand so that you are aware of any current problems that are likely to be raised by callers.

- Don't try to run the programme. You are the expert, but the presenter is responsible for the smooth running of the broadcast.

- Be sympathetic. People only ring in if they feel strongly about things. Thank them for making the call and drawing your attention to the problem. If you alienate them, you may well alienate other listeners.

- Be honest. Explain why things are going wrong, if they are, and say what you are doing about it.

- Don't be afraid to ask questions. Callers may not give the full story. You, too, are entitled to get at the truth.

- You are on the air a long time and listeners tend to stay with Phone-Ins so you have plenty of time to make your points. This sets the Phone-In apart from other interviews.

- Remember, it's informal. Relax and enjoy it.

- Above all put yourself in the shoes of the listener. Most people don't ever ring in to a radio station so it's not something they take lightly and neither should you.

## Press interviews

*"All the political journalists I've met have been piranha fish. However friendly you may feel about them, at the end of the day they look on you as news fodder."* Lord (Ken) Baker, former chairman of the Conservative Party, interviewed in July 2011

The most important difference between broadcast and press interviews is that there is *no performance* when you are talking to a press journalist. This may make the encounter seem less daunting – especially as it will usually take place on the telephone, rather than face-to-face.

Do not be lulled into a false sense of security. Potentially, press interviews are the most dangerous, because:

- They are usually very informal. The journalist will sometimes not seem to be asking questions at all, just making conversation.

- They may last much longer than a broadcast interview, with the journalist exploring many more avenues and asking for a lot more information.

- The journalist is much more likely to talk to a range of other people, with other points of view, some of whom may have more interesting things to say than you.

- You are more likely to be asked 'leading' questions by a journalist who is trying to put words in your mouth – to 'stand up' a particular angle. This process itself is invisible to the audience.

- Your words may look very different in black-and-white. People can't hear your tone of voice, and irony, for instance can be totally lost in print.

- The interview will have a longer 'shelf-life', because news and magazine cuttings are often used for research purposes.

There are some simple rules to follow to reduce risks, and to maximize opportunities presented by a press interview:

- Buy time to prepare. For example say, *"I'd be pleased*

*to talk to you, but I can't at the moment.  Tell me what you need, and I'll get back to you in ten minutes."*

- Follow the same preparation routine as for broadcast interviews.

- Write your key points in large letters on a clean sheet of paper and keep it in front of you throughout the interview – stay focused.

There are many different kinds of journalist, but whether from *The Sun* or *Travel Trade Gazette*, they operate in broadly similar ways.  Never assume that they know what you are talking about.  Always check out that they have understood what you have said.

Never say anything to them, at any time, that you would not be happy to see published on the front page of *The Times!*

Finally, remember that journalists are always on the lookout for a 'good quote'.  It may well influence the way the story is written.  A good press quote follows exactly the same principles as the broadcast soundbite.

Never say anything
to journalists,
at any time, that
you would not
be happy to see
published on the
front page of
*The Times!*

# Chapter 9

## The Soundbite

*"This is not a day for soundbites. But I feel the hand of history upon my shoulder."* Tony Blair, Prime Minister, after signing of Northern Ireland's Good Friday Agreement.

### Packaging of news

In the average TV News bulletin, few items rate more than 1 minute 30 seconds – that's about 340 words maximum.

The report will usually comprise six segments:

1. The 'cue'. The programme presenter introduces the report, including naming the reporter.
2. The 'argument'. The reporter tells us one side of the story.
3. The reporter introduces an interviewee.
4. 'Against' the argument. The reporter tells us the other side of the story.
5. Introduces a second interviewee.
6. Back to the reporter for a conclusion.

There may even be additional interviewees, so the maximum time you are likely to have for your message is 15 seconds. That's 45 words, and that's a soundbite.

On Radio, much the same process occurs, though often the average programme item will be longer – say three minutes. That still leaves you only 30 seconds to get your message across. That's 90 words, and that's a soundbite.

'Clips' will be taken for news bulletins. On commercial radio, especially, these may be as short as 10 seconds. That's 30 words, and that's a soundbite.

**What is a soundbite?**

- The section of your interview which is selected to illustrate the reporter's story.

- The 'best bit' (in the reporter's judgement).

- A memorable quote.

**Why is a good soundbite important to you?**

- It attracts the reporter's attention to what you want to get across.

Sizzling Soundbites!

- It gives you some control over the message(s) selected for inclusion in the story: it should convey your message in a nutshell.

- It makes what you say more accessible and memorable to the audience.

**A good soundbite will be**

- Lively
- Vivid
- Engaging
- Entertaining
- Direct
- Brief

**Creating your soundbite: introducing the 'sizzle' factor**

There are many ways to do this – and broadcasting would be very boring if all soundbites followed exactly the same formula.

However, there are some important elements to consider:

- Flag it up. Draw attention to the important bits of your interview by telling us they are coming up. For example: *"What's really vital here is..."* or *"For me, the really key issue is..."* etc. This also helps ensure that your soundbite is a complete little package.

- Make it self contained. A good soundbite stands alone, without need of the question that elicited it. It will be a complete statement.

- Emphasise it. Use vocal emphasis and put plenty of energy into it, so that it sounds interesting. Even in a press interview, this sends a vital signal to the reporter.

- Give it Impact. Use power words (*huge, vital*) and active verbs, especially if they have emotional content – *hope, inspiration, determination, demand, fight* etc.

- Use word pictures. Analogies, metaphors and similes are useful – people don't need to understand the idea fully, they just know *"it looks like one of these."*

- Use memorable language. Try groups of three ideas – "signed, sealed and delivered", or sequences – past, present and future. You can use repetition to create the group: *"Let's give it a go. Let's back it. Let's try it together."*

- Use compare and contrast: e.g. *"One small step for man, one giant leap for mankind."*

Apply these rules to key points of your interview to produce a 'soundbite' with 'sizzle'! It will be irrisistible to journalists and minimise the risk of the 'wrong bit' being selected. It is more likely to capture the audience's attention too.

**Rehearsal**

The paradox is that if you are really well rehearsed, your soundbite will seem fresher and more powerful. This is because when you come to deliver it, you no longer need to think about the words. Instead, you can concentrate on feeling the emotion. Passion and sincerity are often important elements in a soundbite: they can't be faked, but they can be hidden by the pressure of trying to find the right words.

You should rehearse the phrases you are intending to use as often as possible. Say them out loud, at full volume. Make sure you feel comfortable with them, and the emotions they express. Keep going until they are completely familiar.

*"What we want in 20 seconds is clarity, conciseness and a quick insight into why something is happening."* Alison Sergeant, News Editor, BBC Radio Cambridgeshire

# The Interview
Summary

**Always have something to say – something with impact.**

**Buy time to prepare.**

**Prepare:**

- Who are the AUDIENCE?

- What do I need to tell them? - No more than three MESSAGES

- How can I illustrate – anecdotes, case studies, EXAMPLES

**Predict:**

- NEGATIVE Questions

- Work on a soundbite and rehearse it

**Perform:**

- Energy and Enthusiasm

- Focus

- Acknowledge + Bridge + Content = Control

# Chapter 10

## Managing Your Public Relations

So far, this book has mainly concentrated on your encounters with journalists as an interviewee.  But let us look at media relations in a wider context.

Media interviews and building relationships with journalists will be most effective if they are part of a long-term Public Relations strategy.  It is useful to understand the basics involved in managing your public relations, whether your organisation has an internal PR department, or uses an external PR consultancy – or both, or neither.

**Why it's worth your while to have a strategy**

Research by Virgin on the launch of their financial services company Virgin Finance showed that, pound for pound, money spent on PR was thirty times more effective at generating revenue than that spent on advertising and other paid-for marketing effort. It is significant to note that a communications expert was one of the eight people in the project team which created the company.

*"PR is often under-regarded because it is not associated with big budgets, and it involves risk, not least personal risk for the individual who talks to the media – so this risk needs to be managed".* Rowan Gormley, Managing Director, Virgin Finance

## What would you want PR to do for you?

Take time to think through the answers to these questions:

- What do you hope to achieve by it? (Objectives)
- What do you want to say with it? (Priorities)
- Who do you want to say it to? (Targets)

## PR as part of the marketing mix

Your PR strategy should be broadly in line with your marketing strategy.

> **If a man goes to a party and says to a woman that she needs a man and she should come home with him – that's marketing. If he stands on a chair and announces to the guests his expertise and availability in love – that's advertising. If he tells the woman he is the world's greatest lover and she can't afford to miss the experience – that's selling. But if she comes to him and says that she hears he is the world's greatest lover and would be pleased to come home with him – that's PR!**

**In other words, PR is about awareness ('profile') and reputation.**

Or, as the Chartered Institute of Public Relations would have it:

> *"PR is the deliberate, planned and sustained effort to establish and maintain mutual understanding between an organization and its publics."*

**How this relates to the media**

An effective PR campaign may have elements that are beyond the reach of media exposure – to do with, for instance, customer, staff or parliamentary relations. The importance of media relations is that it can support the other channels of delivery and reach the parts the others don't reach – a mass market.

But remember, your message is always likely to be imprecisely conveyed in the media, because – as we have seen – what you want and what the journalist wants are two different things.

You must present your message in the context of a story. For example, if you want to recruit a new member of staff, that's not likely to be a story, so you will need to place a situations vacant ad. However, if you are recruiting a hundred new people, or if the job is unusual in its context (e.g. a psychologist to deal with stress on the production line), or if you can't find anyone to take the job, despite offering top-rate salary and advertising widely – then you've got a story.

## Getting media attention

The standard way of getting media attention is to send a news release – more commonly known as a press release and these days generally sent electronically. Elsewhere in this book, there is advice about how to put this together [see Chapter 4: *Writing a Good News Release*].

## The obstacles

Every News Desk every day receives scores, sometimes hundreds of releases, many of them professionally produced. More than ninety per cent of them will be deleted or go straight into the waste bin, and every news editor is used to ploughing through Press releases about non-stories. Pity the poor hacks on Shropshire papers who received the following from their local health authority:

> *"Shropshire Health Authority has no comment to make on the comments of the letter about which it was not consulted and which it has not yet seen. Nor do officers of the Health Authority have access to the data upon which the letter is apparently based."*

So, you need to work at getting attention. No, don't try writing on day-glo paper, just remember the most important thing is:

* Have something to say.
* Make sure it's a story.

## Targeting

Knowledge about the readership or audience profiles of the various media outlets is one of the most complex competencies of the PR professional. But there are plenty of common sense decisions to be made about which media might be interested in your story. Local press and radio will want to see the name of their town in the first paragraph. National press will need much more convincing about the strength of the story and its relevance to their readers. Television will want to know what pictures they can get.

If in doubt, try it out by 'selling' your story first. Once you have drafted your ideas, speak to the News Editor of a target publication, or to your journalist 'contact', and tell them you've got a story for them. You might get some useful feedback you can incorporate in the final version. Be prepared to answer the following questions:

• Why should we or our readers care?
• Why is it significant or interesting?
• What are you saying about it?

## Alternatives to the press release

You might get a negative response to the approach described above. This might simply mean you've got the wrong target and you need to try elsewhere. It might mean it is worth trying a different type of approach. The approaches below are not 'second best' and are often more time-effective than writing a news release:

## Comment

If you simply want to get over a message – your 'view' of the world – it is often better to watch out for relevant news stories when they appear, then phone or e-mail a comment on them. Make clear it is for publication. (Along the lines of: Commenting today on the government's decision to raise petrol duty, the RAC said: "*This is another hammer blow against the motorist...*")

## Letters to the Editor

A useful way of introducing ideas to the media environment without having to turn them into stories. They still need to be interesting and relevant, and you still need to have something to say – but the conventions of letter-writing are much more commonplace than news writing. If the letter is interesting enough, you may even find the News Desk follows it up in the form of a story. Warning: You will still be fighting for space – keep it brief, or you will be edited.

## Taking professional advice

Throughout this book, I have encouraged you and your colleagues to get involved in media relations activity, and to play an active part in its management. That is not to say that you should do it on your own. On the contrary, my advice is very clear: whenever you can possibly afford it, take professional advice. It is not necessarily expensive to employ a PR agency for specific campaigns, for instance.

There is good advice available on how to select the right agency for you, from the Public Relations Consultants' Association (PRCA) and from the Chartered Institute of Public Relations (CIPR). [www.prca.org.uk and www.cipr.co.uk].

However, you can use the advice in this book to ensure you get the most from your relationship with the PR professionals. In particular, it is your responsibility to ensure that they have clear guidance on objectives, priorities and targets. Without this, they will be working in the dark.

Have something to say!

Make sure it's a story!

"Pound for pound money spent on PR was thirty times more effective than that spent on advertising".

# Chapter 11

## News Conferences

**When you might consider holding a news conference**

- If an incident or announcement is otherwise likely to create a disruptive level of media inquiries.

- To give senior managers direct access to a wide media audience (and vice-versa).

- To mark the importance of an occasion or of the messages you wish to convey.

- Only hold a News Conference if there is likely to be widespread media interest.

- Do not hold a News Conference as an excuse for holding back information.

**The best time to hold a news conference**

At the earliest opportunity. Given a free choice of times,

11.00 am is often the best compromise between the deadline requirements of evening and morning papers, radio and television. Check for any conflicting media attractions, if you can, and avoid these.

## How to run your News Conference

- Make sure the room is large enough for the numbers expected and well supplied with electric points for TV lights etc.

- Set aside a reasonable area with good sight lines to the platform for photographers and TV cameras.

- Make it clear from the start if there will be any opportunity for separate broadcast interviews. These can be BEFORE or AFTER the News Conference.

- Nominate no more than three platform speakers. They should include the most senior person available and whoever knows most about the subject in hand. You may need further experts close at hand (but not necessarily on the platform).

- The speakers should enter (and later leave) the room through a separate entrance after the media audience has assembled.

- If possible have large clear name cards for each member of the team and make sure your organisation's logo is visible behind them.

- Nominate a Controller who will call in the platform team and then, from the floor, briefly set out the agenda and introduce the speakers. The Controller will keep order, make sure questions are taken fairly and call 'time'. This role is normally taken by a PR professional.

- Speakers should make brief statements (no more than about three minutes) then take questions.

- If there is time, prepare written handouts with facts.

This will avoid time-wasting and help accuracy. You may wish to include a brief statement, which should be vocalised in the introduction to the News Conference, before being handed out.

- Keep it Brief. Normally half an hour or so will be ample. Make this time-frame clear when you call the event, and again at its start.

# Chapter 12

## Crisis and Media Relations

*"When written in Chinese, the word 'crisis' is composed of two characters…one represents danger, the other represents opportunity."*
John F. Kennedy, US President

### Be part of the solution – not the problem

People remember and judge you on how you HANDLE the crisis rather than by the incident itself.  It is important, then, to build media relations into your crisis management communications plan.

- Have a SIMPLE plan in place for reacting to the media in a crisis and make sure it is understood by all managers.

- Begin communicating at once – take the initiative. React quickly but not in panic. Never say "no comment".

- Communicate from the top. Use one named person to co-ordinate media comment. Another named person should act as spokesman and should be a senior member of the organisation.

- Be HONEST but POSITIVE, not defensive.

- Control the flow of information by releasing statements at predetermined times. These should be set by you – but try to accommodate journalists' deadlines.

- Consider calling a News Conference so that all journalists' questions can be dealt with at once – but remember in an ongoing incident regular updates will be required.

- Treat all media seriously and don't neglect any outlet, especially those in your sphere of operation, including the regional press where you are situated.

**In case of emergency break glass**

Here is a quick and easy guide to what to say in emergency. When preparing to talk to the media, rather than asking yourself the question "What can I tell them?" think about "What needs to be said here?"

You may be surprised to know that it will always be the same, or similar during the crucial early stages of crisis. Base them on the acronym CARE. Whatever the crisis, your media statements should always include elements of the following:

# Concern

Have sympathy for the point of view of those adversely affected – protesters or families of bereaved, for example.

# Action

Your audience needs to know you will be doing something, even if it is only an internal inquiry.

# REASSURANCE

For example, state that lessons will be learned and/or that you have a good safety/security record and contingency plans.

**Find out more about crisis communications in our companion guides:**

*Risk Issues and Crisis: Managing threats to your reputation* and *Case Studies in Risk Issues and Crisis Communications*

# Chapter 13

## The Future of Media:
## Convergence and Conversation

Much has changed on the media scene in the past 20 years, the rate of change is accelerating, and even more will change in the next ten years. This has tremendous implications for the PR professionals and others who have to deal with the media.

The advent of 'new media' – digital distribution, online news and information, blogs and social networking – is not only a phenomenon in its own right, but is also changing the nature of the traditional media.

Newspapers and magazines have increasingly become an online resource. Print circulations generally decline, while essentially the same product grows its readership online. The online versions, of course, can have more depth ('linking' to similar or background stories, for instance). They can also include non-print elements (online video, for example, a process known as 'convergence'). Equally, a broadcast story becomes a print story (on the BBC website, for instance). And there is much more space and opportunity for 'reader comment' and other interactivity – far beyond the traditional and limited 'Letters' page.

Media outlets still struggle with how to 'monetise' the internet, as advertising spend is spread ever more thinly. Terrestrial TV and radio stations face massively increased competition for audience time thanks to multi-channel digital broadcasting via satellite, digi-box or DAB.

It is much too early, and probably wrong, to predict the death of newspapers. The total circulation of UK National newspapers alone still stands at 11-million. And research suggests that stories still tend to carry more influence in the political and business worlds when they are taken up by the traditional media.

However, there are some crucial structural and operational changes to the media world which cannot be ignored by anyone seeking to communicate with a wider audience:

- Newspaper and magazine websites are increasingly embracing podcasting (audio reports and interviews), video podcasting ('vodcasting') or streamed video reports. More and more non-media websites also use these channels of communication. The skills of the TV interview are therefore becoming an essential skill for managers.

- In many fields, leading bloggers are becoming as

influential as any traditional writer.  Already, many major companies (e.g. in the electronics sector) are treating key bloggers as seriously as traditional media outlets, inviting them to press conferences, launches etc.

- Social networking sites and online chat groups mean a return to the principles of conversation with your audience – communication is no longer a one-way street.  Organisations and individuals will have to adapt to the loss of control and deference inherent in this.

- Online conversations (e.g. via Twitter) have become a major source of stories for traditional media too.  This, too, is a two-way process: journalists use Twitter to ensure they are first and fast with the news.  It is now possible (and legally sanctioned) for journalists to tweet verdicts, sentences etc. direct from inside a court-room, for example.

The good news is that the basic principles of effective communication remain the same, and all the rules, hints and tips in this book therefore still apply.  Perhaps the changing scene simply gives new emphasis to the rubric of *putting the audience first*.

So it's not case of, "What do we want to tell them?" but "What do they need to hear from us?"

**Other titles in this series**

Risk Issues and Crisis: Managing threats to your reputation by Magnus Carter

Case Studies in Risk Issues and Crisis Communications by Magnus Carter

Get the Presentation X Factor! by Tina Coulsting Carter